GOOD TO BE ME
My Gratitude Journal

By RA Cook

Illustrations by Mike Quinones G

With every step I take,
I choose to look for what is great.
One step at a time, mile after mile,
I can find so many things, that make me smile.
It is fun to search, it is important to me,
to share with my gratitude journal, all I see.

"You're always with yourself so you might as well enjoy the company."

Diane Von Furstenberg

What Makes You Smile?

⭐ _____
_____
_____

⭐ _____
_____
_____

⭐ _____
_____

"Because of you, I laugh a little harder, cry a little less, and smile a lot more."

Unknown

Who do you like to spend time with and what do you enjoy doing with them?

Fall Seven Times, Stand Up Eight

Japanese Proverb

What are things you can count on or like to do when you have a tough or sad day?

_____
_____
_____
_____
_____
_____
_____
_____
_____
_____

Your challenge today is to go through your day with a grateful heart, notice what makes you happy, anything that makes you smile.
You can draw a picture about something you appreciate.

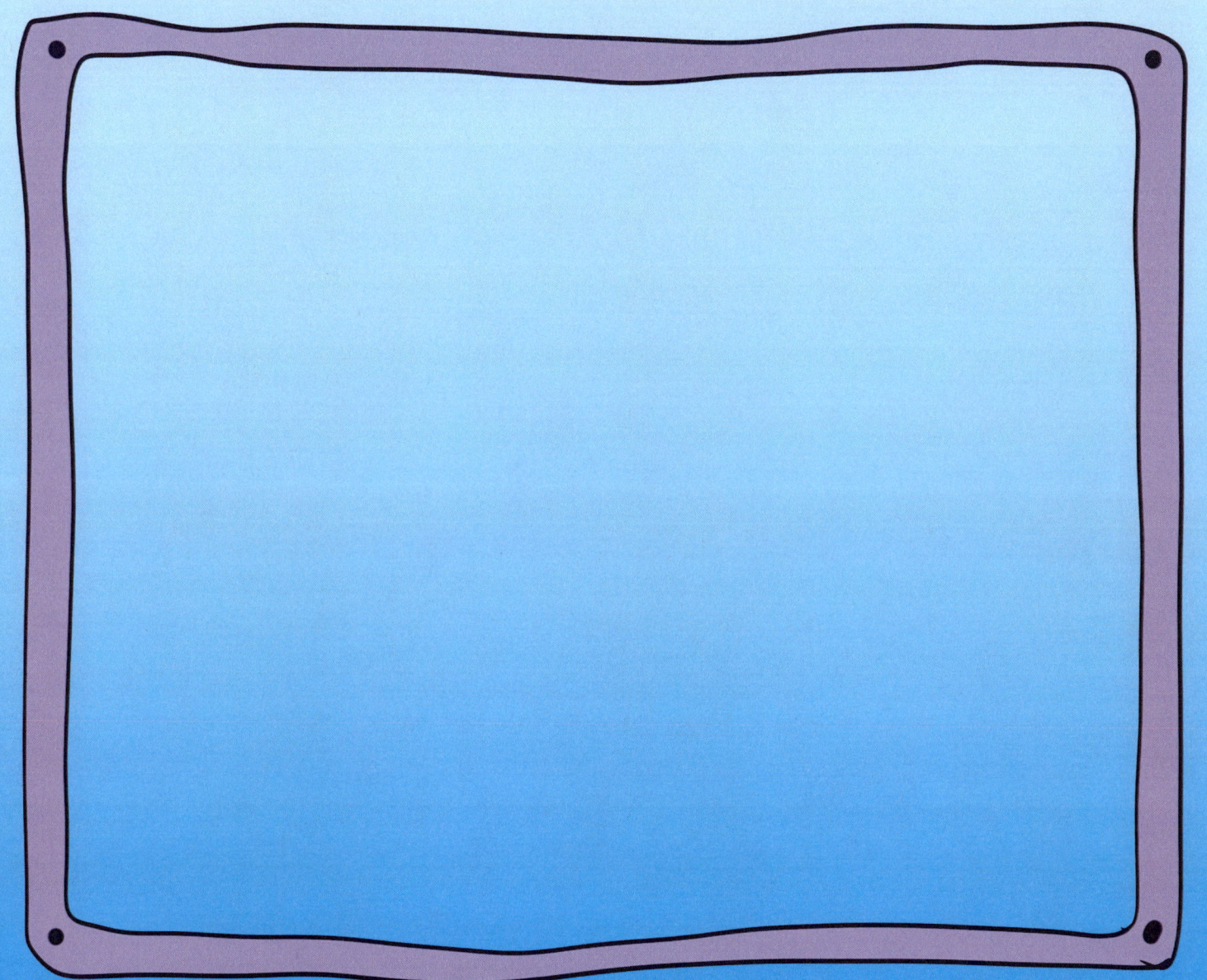

My Gratitude Journal Begins

Today's Date _____

_____
_____
_____
_____
_____

_____
_____
_____
_____

_____
_____
_____
_____

Today's Date _____

Date _____

_____

_____

_____

_____

_____

Date _____

_____

_____

_____

_____

_____

_____

Today's Date _____

Today's Date _____

Date _____

_____

_____

_____

_____

_____

_____

Date _____

Date _____

_____

_____

_____

_____

_____

Today's Date _____

_____
_____
_____
_____

_____
_____
_____
_____

_____
_____
_____
_____

_____
_____
_____
_____

Date _____

_____

_____

_____

_____

_____

_____

Date _____

Date _____

_____

_____

_____

_____

_____

Date _____

_____

_____

_____

_____

_____

Today's Date _____

Today's Date _____

_____
_____
_____
_____

_____
_____
_____
_____

_____
_____
_____
_____

_____
_____
_____
_____

Date _____

Date _____

_____

_____

_____

_____

_____

Date _____

Date _____

_____

_____

_____

_____

_____

_____

Date _____

_____

_____

_____

_____

_____

_____

Date _____

_____

_____

_____

_____

_____

_____

Today's Date _____

_____
_____
_____
_____

_____
_____
_____
_____

_____
_____
_____
_____

_____
_____
_____
_____

Today's Date _____

Date _____

_____

_____

_____

_____

_____

Date _____

_____

_____

_____

_____

_____

_____

Date _____

Today's Date _____

_____
_____
_____
_____

_____
_____
_____
_____

_____
_____
_____
_____

_____
_____
_____
_____

Date _____

_____

_____

_____

_____

_____

_____

Date _____

_____

_____

_____

_____

_____

_____

Date _____

Today's Date _____

To everyone who has filled my gratitude journal with your smiles, laughter, friendship, and love-this book is dedicated to you. Special thanks to Sarah Ban Breathnach, author of Simple Abundance, and Oprah Winfrey, who taught me the life-changing power of capturing gratitude each day.

I'd love for you to explore the other books in the Good To Be Me series. According to my dogs, they're must-reads--and I trust their judgment completely.

Good To Be Me - Discovering What Makes Me Special & Unique
Good To Be Me - The Coloring Book
Good To Be Me - The Gratitude Journal

RA Cook is a writer, podcast host, leadership coach, human resources advisor, traveler, foodie, kindness advocate and lifelong learner. She is always on the lookout for new places, ideas and adventures to explore and enjoy with family and friends. RA believes our experiences, conversations and smiles connect us and help to bring out the best in each other.

RA is the author of five star rated book series – *Good To Be Me – Discovering What Makes Me Special & Unique*, guiding kids to begin discovering and developing their life story in clever, fun ways.

RA is the host and executive producer of *Well Done You*, a popular podcast featuring engaging guests and conversations. Listeners describe it as refreshing, heartfelt, and entertaining. Well Done You is available wherever you listen to podcasts.

A New England native, RA raised her family in North Florida. She enjoys life with her treasured tribe and the three best dogs in the world – Bella, Charlie Bean & Oliver. Follow RA on social media @RACook, subscribe to our podcast Well Done You and visit our website www.racookieproductions.com

Mike Quinones G, a Colombian born artist, who has worked as a profesional illustrator since he was 15 years old. Raised in Miami, he has been able to absorb the city's diversity. Now he resides in Nashville TN, where he is able to surround himself with the most talented artists, who give him his inspiration.

www.ingramcontent.com/pod-product-compliance
Lightning Source LLC
Chambersburg PA
CBRC090843120626
46551CB00009B/745

*9 7 9 8 9 9 3 3 8 6 2 1 8 *